I0749979

REFLECTIONS ON CHROME
Parking Lot Confessions in Poetic Prose

by Branch Isole

REFLECTIONS ON CHROME
Parking Lot Confessions in Poetic Prose
by Branch Isole

Printed in the United States of America

Library of Congress Control Number:
2005936871
ISBN 0-9747692-5-8

Mana'o Publishing
PO Box 1696
Lahaina, HI 96767-1696

My poetry is inspired by the Hula.
The Hula is precise, sensual, sexual
and sophisticatedly raw as it tells a story.
I am a voyeur of the Hula for all its character.

The poems herein are short stories of
issues and emotions surrounding personal
responsibility choice and avoidance.
This is 'Voyeurism Poetry'.

Reflections on Chrome contains adult material
and language, some of which is sexual in nature.
It is intended for mature audiences only.

Contents

Introduction

Everyone has a story to tell. Issues and events become the tenor of our lives. Most are told and retold to friends, then to acquaintances and eventually to anyone who will listen.

These intimate late night lamentations between friends often hold the greatest amount of truth and pain. With the first telling, the raw emotions of the experience and the people involved are exposed without the machinations of embellishment or feigned pity. It is from this initial spark of conversation the story takes on its ability to grow in many different directions, infused with a myriad of festering thoughts and feelings.

All over our world tonight, best friends are hearing for the first time, stories of life's emotional traumas. Many are taking place as parking lot confessions.

Branch Isole

"Living is easy with eyes closed
Misunderstanding all you see"

-Lennon/McCartney-
from
"Strawberry Fields Forever"
on
'Magical Mystery Tour'

Cherie

Harassing her daily
part and parcel
of their ride home
in the belly of the yellow beast
Two little Jonahs
with nothing more to do
than torment a girl
named Cherie

The goal,
leave her crying
by the time she stepped off the bus
We did our clowning
while in her tears
she'd be drowning

Called her 'the chow'
Each time I remember it now
on these long and lonely
afternoons
it is my heart that breaks,
aches

Pre-teen boys
with an exuberance of ignorance
and cruelty shown
toward one who wanted only
to be left alone

I hope she's there
to see us flogged
through our embarrassment
and shame
For the terrible things
we said and claimed
and the horrible ways
we criticized
her being and her name

I hope she's there to see
the skin stripped from our backs
With a sense of vengeance
and revenge,
for the kindness
and compassion
we both did lack

I hope through our anguish
she obtains relief
and for our childish pranks
we are adopted by her grief

The thing is,
when our day finally comes
and we are presented
as the arrogant and selfish ones
we were back then
on so many an afternoon,
my guess is
instead of our doom

Cherie will be standing
in a forgiving light
emanating strength
from a thousand points
of love's majestic might

She'll be there
the innocent and beautiful one
and all will see
she has finally won

My guess is
she'll overlook
what inconsiderate bastards
were we
For neither then nor now
could we live up to
the character of Cherie

Closed Doors

Behind closed doors
where prying eyes can't go
lurk motives and behaviors
hidden from public view
Good, bad and ugly
dwell within

Harm and love abound
in varying degrees
among young and old alike
both male and female types,
from terrible violence
to petty gripes

We are shocked to discover
beneath our neighbor's pleasant veneer
lives and breathes a monster,
next door
down the block
ever so near

Facade and mask
correctly in place
hiding
covering
veiling the face

The one which lies
to others,
to self

One put up on
and taken down
off the shelf

Drama stricken
Living in fear
Fear of discovery
Fear of the truth
Fear of calling
a spade a spade
Moving forward
while whitewashing stains
of a life in retrograde

Aware an illness
does exist
Using rationalization
Claiming victimization
Denying responsibility
Controlling every fix

The person
The couple
The family,
most likely to what?
Succeed
Succumb
Perpetrate
Perpetuate
Escape, from themselves?

Crowded Nest

Blank mind, black
Blank page, white
Empty slate, writer's block
Pinpoint, tunnel's light
Seedling thought

Germinating words, unknown
Hidden points of view
Shades and shadows overwhelm
masked, veiled,
shrouded lightly
struggling to bloom

Expressions, expressly
begging to be freed
Stumbling, tumbling
desiring egress
Forming cohesive word order
on paper's placement
from mind's crowded nest

A poem exists somewhere therein
for lyricist's poetic mind
never really rests

It's goal, divulge
once again
better
better
best

Oh covetous, elusive words
soaring beyond mind's reach
Beseeching they become
parts of lines
to stretch
grow
and weave

Into tales
to be told
of adventures brave,
and ventures bold

Cruelty of Age

His libido has died
but he’s still alive
What a cruel joke to play
on adulthood
Now it becomes clearer
when they declare
‘Youth, is wasted on the young’

Discipline's Disciple

He was just
who he was
parenting skills
learned and passed on
Abuse and mayhem
disguised and labeled
discipline,
the cycle unbroken

The first time
they saw him
he slept on the couch,
that was at
her grandparents' house

Staring blankly
at the stranger
Then,
at each other
Who was this man?
They would ask
her mother

Recollection was
his anger cursed
with four letter words
interspersed

He was just
who he was
parenting skills
learned and passed on

Putting his hand
through the window pane
By his tirade orated
you'd thought him a man
gone insane

Abuse and mayhem
disguised and labeled
discipline,
the cycle unbroken

Anger and frustration
grew inside,
while those around him
learned to hide

He was just
who he was
parenting skills
learned and passed on

Moments of compassion?
There was one or two
but in four thousand days
that's relatively few

Abuse and mayhem
disguised and labeled
discipline,
the cycle unbroken

For those there companioned
who knew his fists well
life under his roof
was a living hell

The day he died
was bittersweet
Parting years earlier
separation
now hung in the air
still incomplete

She went to see him
the other day
to forgive,
and simply to say

Staring blankly at the marker
whispering under her breath
to the one now held
firmly by death

"You were just
who you were
parenting skills
learned and passed on
Abuse and mayhem
disguised and labeled
discipline,

the cycle now broken"

Disrespect

With augmentation to your breasts
you now have two perfect
spherical orbs
nestled on your rib cage
riding high upon your chest

It doesn't get
any better than this

Beneath a plunging
scoop neck sheath
as thin as a shadow
hidden in view
by a single layer
of lustrous material
Erect nipples stand
as if brushed by a cool breeze
to interrupt and support
faux silk that flows
Simultaneously
hanging and clinging
it glides to and fro

A style designed
for a romantic eve's quest
glides as water lapping gently
against two areola capped
tide riding buoys
on a sea of flesh

When you scrutinize yourself
in front of your baroque framed
full length mirror
prior to stepping out
into the public domain
are you aware of your appearance?

Or is the sensual attire
accenting your longing gaze
mistakenly thrust
out of place?

We query your steely-eyed glare
aimed in our direction
as our sights were drawn to you
true was your perception
Is your presentation of self
intended to compel
awe struck croonery?
Or are we to ignore your presence
leaving you cloistered
in private oblivion
and self-centered buffoonery?

You can't have it both ways

You glance back
over your shoulder
piercing
with self-absorbed assertions
to determine if we
continue to stare

At the patch of denim
you've chosen to wear
Which you portend to pass off
as a covering for cheeks
exposed explicitly bare

Armed with your look
to entrap
the same one you used
at your approach
Insuring we noticed
the splayed front flap
triangulated between zipper and pockets

Resembling a double knit suit's
wide open lapels
the metal teeth pointing
to your muffled pelt
With so much pubic bone
brazenly exposed
a finger tip's insertion
would have brushed
your swollen clit's dome

Yes, we saw
we're gaping still
Isn't that what you want?
Isn't that why you flaunt?
Why not simply wear a thong
as the streetwalkers do?

Oh, that isn't you?

True,
at least the hooker
has the courtesy
to be real,
getting paid for that
she's compelled to do
What about you?

Do you want us to look
Or not?. . . .Well, do you?
Which will it be?

You can't have it both ways

Hey there little mama
We see you're expecting
Congrats!

How did we know?

Perhaps it was your exposed
expanding womb
Basking prodigiously
out front it protrudes,
nakedly leading your way

An epidermal bow
acting as the plow
cutting through the atmosphere
burrowing through the thoroughfare
Occupying the area
of your impending approach

As effective as a locomotive's
bare cow-catcher
Clearing the way
Announcing your arrival
Heralding your coming

Now don't misjudge
or mistake
We're happy for your current state
and you certainly have that pre-natal glow
but it's a shame
you've chosen to stain
nature's aura
in a blatant disregard
for common decency
to placate your insecure ego

Having the need to proclaim
your motherhood aloud
Is it also necessary to expose it
totally bare
to an otherwise, adoring crowd?

This pregnancy may be your first
but Believe It Or Not, as Ripley would say
You're not the first
to be in 'the way'

Please show your unborn child
some dignity and reserve
by covering, him or her

Ladies, respect yourself!
Don't present us you
as a piece of meat
or an object of temporary
temporal desire,
to be used, abused
then discarded on the heap
of past mistakes'
burning pyre

What you project
is how you're perceived
What you send out
is what we receive

Emote Motif

So,
How does it feel
to be nothing more
than an afterthought?
A visual question mark?
What it is like
to be seen
walking behind a woman
who deems herself,
Queen

One who by the surgeon's skills
so brazenly
and overtly endowed
appears to be carrying
below her chin
two inflated utters
from a Guernsey cow

So,
How does it feel
insecure man
in this day and time
Heeling to her self believed
false regalia
while walking two steps behind?

Our compliments
to her plastic surgeon
yes that's quite a rack
but doesn't all the extra weight
put a strain upon her back?

Is she as insecure today
as in the moments before
her massive physical transformation?
And did it accomplish
all that was meant
for her mind and body relation?

So,
How does it feel
to be the secondary sight
An object of scorn
jealousy and laughter
As you my man trail behind
and skip, merrily after?

Do you purposely stay
at arm's length away
while in her flowing wake?
The one that ebbs
she thinks,
a presence does it make

So,
How does it feel
Avoiding her eyes,
those that dart and stray
While yours remain focused
on the back of her head,
that you might crawl inside
each night,
while being in her bed?

Our compliments
to her plastic surgeon
he accomplished quite a feat,
when was the last time standing erect
she actually saw her feet?

So,
How does it feel
to know she's casting
alternating glances
of seduction and daggers,
at those who stop and stare
Seen and known
by your heart
Surely you're aware?

So,
How does it feel
Do you ever worry
she may curtly mention
she's leaving you for another,
one who adores her more
Dare you tire
of making her
your idol of attention?

So,
Has she grown weary
of never being looked in the eye
As strangers she and you pass by
ask themselves,
then wonder why?

Our compliments
to her plastic surgeon
she obviously wants
the world to stare,
but my friend
the reality is
the world doesn't care

So,
How does it feel
to appear the lackey
porter of her baggage
wherever she does roam

Waiting upon haltered staggering steps
as she slows to survey
all she mentally owns

We strictly ask
from clinical curiosity
How does it feel
to walk daily behind
a man made mammary monstrosity?

Escape

Out of the bouquet
of day lilies
All of whom wait patiently
expecting soon to die
One seemingly peeks over
the terra cotta rimmed vase
out of its familial
splash of colors
red, yellow, fuchsia

All but one
bursts up and out
All but one
seeks light and warmth

In their imminent demise
the promise of a second life
To be trimmed
and gathered
for future's present

To be dried and lacquered
that they may perhaps
brighten the table
with but a muted resemblance
of what once they were
separately, together

One alone casts
its failing energies
downward
as if planning its escape
prior to that predestined place
upon the mantel
under the proud bull elk

Fit To Be Tied

I don't think
I want to be spanked
I'm all grown up now
too big for that
After all, I'm as lean
as old Jack Sprat
and a good sexual whipping
would touch me
to the bone
(and I can only have
that much fun,
away from home)

Please don't hurt me
I can't stand the pain,
No harder still
make my butt burn and sting
with redness
from your crop
from your whip
from your leather baton toy
I need to be punished
I've been such a bad boy

To control me
with your crop
your whip
your big black wooden paddle
would take me back
in my head,
behind those sacred curtains

I'd feel Father Old Leery's
warm nicotine breath
and hear his old brogue prattle,
confusing me
abusing me
accusing me
of being so bad,
so good,
I'd be wishing again
he could, he would,
wait, maybe not
I'm not really sure
I'm not really me
I'm trapped

Oh you,
you've got me so addled

Frustration

The most frustrating times
Jesus ever faced
had nothing to do
with the cross
or saving
a sinful human race

If His days were
anything like ours
His greatest task
daily was found
dealing with self-centered hypocrites
from sun up, to sun down

His tests of faith
were not in belief,
Was He or Was He Not?
regarding His role
as savior,
His faith was grilled
with regularity
by acts of self-indulgence
and its corresponding behavior

These He accepted as part of the job
Understanding man's selfishness
'goes with the territory'
you might say,
same as today

The one that required
His patience in this life
was confronting self-righteous people
of every stripe

In virtually every instance
of contact He had
He was kind
and gentle
and seldom walked away mad
However, even He became frustrated
with mankind's propensity
for selfish impropriety

He never responded
with hate or revenge
or a pharisaic 'Jonesing' one-up-manship
Nor did He ever reply
in a tone of sass or lip
He would suggest
"those who have ears,
let them hear"

"Love and truth
and compassion, please
It is with these
you will win your release"

Now realize,
understand
and marvel at,
in every instance

His response was consistent
Never giving up
giving in
or shouting ‘get a grip’

Never chiding with a yell
‘go to hell’

Never asking
‘now really, please’
Never exclaiming
‘give me a break’

Forgiveness was exhaled
in every breath
He did take

Want to use Jesus
as your example today
of true Spiritual Christianity?
Then every single time
someone makes
a bone head mistake
or does something idiotic
or is selfish and rude
Stop,
and truly remember
what Jesus would do

Game Day

Riding,
on a bench of existence
Waiting,
in and out of sight
Praying,
the coach will put me in
Afraid,
he might

Testing,
self effacing efforts
with a broad stroke brush
Painting,
a scene for public consumption
and critique

Anticipation
Agitation
Deep down
No, deeper still
In a place as dark
as black hole's night
Raw nerves flutter
coveys of synapse butterflies,
taking flight

Readied
for first contact strike,
I am born

Going Going Done

Ran out of words
starting this poem

Guess this is
as far as it's going

Heartfelt

Fulfillment of the heart
with the coveted things
of this world
is reflected in such as;
size, color and cost
Blinding us to Him
who truly fulfills,
and may be eternally lost

Held

The one who fears death
has yet to grasp,
Belonging to the creator
is an eternal connection
of soul to Spirit
held tight from first to last

Physical realities held within
the realms of time and space
Existing that each being may grow
closer to God
and in its day
see His face

Birth relinquishes not
obligations
for each and every
sojourned soul
Neither through its liberation
nor material quest
To be held by the light of God
is eternal life,
not eternal rest

Searching for identity
in times before
as now
Truths held out
for each to know
part and parcel
of moral indemnity

God's granted opportunities,
lessons and experiences
reliant upon understanding of truth
Tests and trials
Choices between
self and unconditional love
by His living proof

Aligned betwixt
thought and breath
each mortal being must acquiesce
An eternal soul
held as example for us
by His truth
His love
His trust

How Do Stars Pop the Question

Do they ask?
Do they tell?
Do they open a vein
and start to bleed?
Do they obtain a script
from which to read?
Do they take lightly
their newly beloved's
nubile hand
and with their celebrity
regally command?

The headline posited,
boasted it,
oh so querily,
then proceeded
to explain
'verily, verily'
Stating it's different
than for you or me

So where is this line
between rich and poor
For many it's the one
between spending
and doing time

How much stuff
How many toys
have you in store?
At a minimal
I'm expecting continually
at least one more

Stating clearly
with 'them'
it's different
than for you or I
Of course our egos
need not be stroked so high

As if to verify
this time anew
through his grand intentions
Validating for the world to see
a picture of her oh,
so beautiful ring
It's glittering elegance
evidence
of the song within his heart
once more does it sing

Oh to be privy
with numbers one and two
Wondering
and hearing knowledge
only they once knew
For lust is lust
ask any ex-es
The apex where past wives'
camaraderie
meets at its nexus

The medias' persistent focus again
for the Nth time today
brought to our attention
neither quote nor word
were they to say

Shall we go beyond
numbers one and two,
why not add one more
For all Hollywood
and beyond
knew of three who did lose,
Misses Cruise, Cruise and Cruz

Identity Theft

So I just had to ask
"What's the meaning
of all those tattoos?"
"Damn" he replied,
"I wish I knew,
I did, sort of
with the first one or two,
then it became a habit
a phase you might say
I thought I'd grow through"

"But I didn't
I wouldn't
I couldn't quit,
and after a while
I didn't give a shit,
as too how ridiculous
how uncontrolled
circus-like, I appeared
With each new one
my insecurities grew
as did my fears"

"My body took on
a life of it's own
and my commands
it began
to dethrone"

“All it wanted
was more and more ink
with each new ‘tat’
on the edge, on the brink”

“Graven and craven images
fought for virgin skin
Demanding attention
Adding commentary
to rival the others
in a battle of prominence
and placement to win”

“And what of you,
your mind, your soul?”
“Me,” he replied
“I just don’t know”

“What more can I do
except to give in
and allow colored ink
to take over my skin”

“The only alternative
to erase these images
blurring with age
like mottled tar,
is to trade them in
for laser scars”

"You see my friend
I'm at their mercy
and as much as I wish
to make my amends
my deep rooted insecurities
require I remain
a living canvas
enslaved by them"

In the Breach

For each of us
thrown over for another
At least one persistent
burning question remains
while wondering about
our formers new lover.

What are they like?
What is it they have?
that makes us
our formers last?

With all our queries
our doubts
our fears
the sole true reason
we are brought to tears

One simple fact
remains the crux
steeping out
of relationship dust,
the great transgression
is abuse of the trust.

Influential Sorts

Each learns
from those they see
their icons of endearment,
whom it is
they wish to be

Our emulation of what?
Which part of the whole?
What percentage of "them"
do we desire
to grasped in our hold?

Masters, Teachers
Preachers
of enlightenment
Leader who would be king
Each of us caught in a trap
one of our own making

Future's visionary
Lyrically scripted
Portrayed in the arts
Fantasy fears
played out
in the dark

Beginning to end
days, months, years
eclipsing times, emotional mind bend

Modern day Columbus'
roaming the world free
attempting to prove
earth's flat edge
mere illusion,
not reality

Influential sorts
groundwork and paths
do they lay

Insatiable Sex Bum

Falling in love
several times a day
as attractive persons
of the opposite sex
into my field of vision do stray
Looking joyfully
with a full-on gaze
natural and assisted beauties abound
dare I say

On further reflection
it's more likely lust
The mental gymnastics
which toy with my mind,
as I imagine
time after time
with this one, with that
so many to choose from
if my fantasies were real
my title would be
'insatiable sex bum'

At the end of the day
I return home to my spouse
the one whose life I share
day in and day out
The attraction's still there,
a little tempered, slightly numb
but then kicks in salacious visions
for this, insatiable sex bum

My spouse has changed
over the years
but then so have I
I'm no longer svelte
with petite waist and abs
and this muscle tone
has turned mildly to flab

Part of the process
known as age
we share together
as the book of our life
keeps turning each page

It's my spouse who truly
gets my attention
because that which we share
goes deeper than skin
It's emotional
fulfillment
strong
and clear
It's honest
tight
true
and sincere

It's with my spouse
I can be all I dare
For us,
it's long term
desire and care

Sure, we could cheat
stumble and fall,
lie and deceive
and forfeit it all
And then what?
Start ‘fresh’
with someone new
for the sake of a thrill
or a fantasy screw
In an attempt
to establish what?
love, hope and trust
driven by
and grown out of lust?

Think I’ll go home
to that spouse of mine
and rekindle once more
love and lust
with my long term best friend,
the one I know will be there
right up ‘til the end

I’ll avoid all the fuss
and keep those fantasies fun
focused and honed
on the one
with whom I have all
so we both can enjoy
this insatiable sex bum

for CC

It's Hard

It's hard
being away
from the one you love
Even harder
when you're not sure
do they feel the same
Can they be trusted
you ask yourself
when this is the case

Each day drags on
while you wish it would race,
and bring forth the time
when you two will be back together again

Or so you think…

Do you really want to know?
Is that why you rehearse
over and over
in your head
the things you'll say
when you're back in bed

You hope so, right?

but what if they are with
another tonight?

If that's so
then why the mental trip,
Is that why
you continue to rip
the spirit from your soul,
torturing yourself
about what you believe
you should be feeling,
and what you've been told

Can they be trusted?
Can you?
So far apart
what will you do?

Pine and opine
over what you may learn
Anxiously anticipating
agonizing
crying
over the truth
of why you two
are apart,

it's all a matter
of the heart

Latté Chat

A din of voices
fills the background
The dull roar of white noise
doth abound

Multitudes of stories
being explained in detail

Who did what,
to whom
and why

Speculating
where it will land them
in the end,
and when

Contemporary commentaries
on other peoples lives,
as if it mattered to them

Carnal knowledge
Joy in the exchange
of retelling again and again

"Oh to be a fly on the wall"
the related common thread
of comic oral text

Discussing carnival outcomes
Who in the process
will be hurt next

Prurient interests and desires
vociferously proclaimed
As conversations
revolve around chronicles
of lies, sex and pain

Speaking in deft tones,
hushed veils
truncate the bleed
Removing meat
from the bones
Wallowing in
their frenzied feed

Leaving others
to their demise
hanging unmasked,
Skeletons in the closets

Living Loving Memory

Leaving hearts behind broken
in these mourning moments of time
Grief weighs immeasurably down
upon these present
emotions and minds

Sensing your spirit
among us once more
Our loss overwhelming,
yet put away. .

By remembrance of your smile
ever brightly beaming

Your body at rest
Your soul gliding free
Peace now shrouding protectively
the new essence of your being
Your time here so fleetingly passed
still hard to imagine you're gone
In glory waiting patiently
for our journey's end . .
to join you before the throne

Lost in Thought

Cast upon the breadth of the universe

Elation dawning
Awakened
hand in hand
Quietly bursting forth
upon the landscape of reality

As if materializing
from the void,
a catalytic explosion
of the soul's "big bang"

Moving along synapse paths
merging from an on-ramp
of mentality
at the speed of thought

Recognition of its energy
revealing both
creator and utilitarian placement
The seed sowing alteration
on one of life's travails
has occurred

Originality dwarfed
by connection
to the already existent,

originality, with a little "o"

Menopause

Having endured
all the suffering
men can cause
There's a reason
it's called
men o pause

Obit

The clouds creep in
like death,

To sleep
To dream
To live

where,
and for how long?

In what method of madness
lies your demise
Given the choice
which would you revise

Never thinking
their names would appear
printed on a page this way
Never,
never in a lifetime,
in *USA Today*

Sandwiched between
topics of terror
and auto promo ads
Their few lines
without error
exposing trauma
experienced by soldiers four,
as each crossed over
and through death's door

Oedipus Revisited

Discovering you
could be a full time chore
Finding your line
between Madonna and whore
For my fantasies are
oh so pendular
and yet, I find
none regrettable
Although I do struggle
with those
which are Oedipal

One Bottle of Beer, One Cup of Coffee

This world over
two men sit
sharing thoughts
of days past
Events they swore
would ne'er be forgotten
Times they believed
which would always last

Against a backdrop
of what once was reality
blended memories blur
Trying now to recall
adventures, escapades, stories
Moments of pain
Moments of glory

Those which have become
both faded
and exaggerated
Struggling for their rightful place
Fighting for their existence
like World War II's celebrated
insurgent resistance

Each mind's exercise
Each day's attempts to revive
Long awaited
and remembered dreams
Those which once were,
are still,
and hope yet to be seen

And all the while
each soul marches
stealthily onward
Its singular goal
to be washed clean

Each picture
Every line
All etchings,
Clean slate
Preparations for
a new birth arrival
at heaven's gate

Parousia Timetable

Walking the plank
one of wormwood hewn
void of love
Alternating footfalls
some smooth
others rough

When will my time come
Father,
"Fear not my son,
soon enough"

Immersion into the abyss
of man and his makings
Watching hands grasp
all to be had
all to be taken
Fight or flight instincts
genetic predisposition of survival
What of their spiritual loss?
What of their souls' revival?

When will my time come
Father,
"Fear not my son,
soon enough"

Your presence arrives
from behind the blind spot
Yea, do emerge
Plant seeds of awareness
Seeds of light
within the darkened shroud
Seeds of acknowledgment
of eternal life
all to be sung aloud
Into hearts
hardened so tough

When will my time come
Father,
“Fear not my son,
soon enough”

Personal Resolution

Poetry, regardless of form
by its very nature
is meant to spark
universal emotions
common to personal resolution
Not merely to describe the author's
daily constitution

Private Cell Phone
Public Conversation

Dizzily confused
I wait for you,
wait for you
to make up your mind,
about me
about us
no regrets
no fuss,
just tell me please
say which way
it's to be,
will we be free
free one from the other
freedom done
freedom won
free to go on
to the next
to another
one

Waiting by the phone
waiting all alone
waiting on words
words from you,
words of relief
words of elation
words,
of celebration
words turned blue

I wish now I knew. . .
or do I?

What to do
waiting,
waiting,
waiting on you

One ring
two, three
now four
Do I act aloof
needing no proof,
proof we are both
about to lose

“Hello,
oh, it’s you
ok
fine
I sort of knew
Well,
we both need
a fresh start
a new me
a new you,
Yes, I understand
of course I do
it’s ok
I’m all grown up
just like you

No, I'll be fine
sure, maybe a little blue
but don't worry
I'll get over you
just like you already have
No problem my love
Good luck ,
you too
Goodbye"

you schmuck

Purpose

Everything in nature
serves a purpose

Man's blessing and bane
is to be the one creature
who can sense
the purpose served,
is to come closer to God
and to His Word

Life's credibility built
one statement at a time,
searching;
one thought remembered

Not knowing its import
or longevity,
while seldom realizing,
what it will be

All wanting approval,
need,
for and from others
family, friends, lovers

REM

Prone position anticipated
Pressure released
Tension gone
Stress all but eliminated
Hard stiff body
enveloped within the folds
Brain and heart pulsating
as if both might explode
With an initial
and simultaneous last
elongated stretch
A sigh is reaped
as her head
hits the pillow
Overtaking her exhaustion
is REM sleep

Her body supine
the closing doors of her mind
shut out
the light of the day
and in its place of dominance seeps
clouds of desires unfulfilled
which float and billow
across the landscape of her dreams

Repentance

"Am I to stand trial?"
tentatively she asked
with doe eyed innocence
so long ago practiced
and perfected
Her feigned look
at the ready,
the one she uses if ever
she's rejected

"Trial" he responded
"Oh no,
Nothing quite so dramatic
Nothing quite so traumatic"

"Your soul atonement
to be made today
is only for those sins
made along the way
Temptations you gave into
Those you traversed
while waiting for this day
on mother earth"

"Those committed
after repentance
Those which tempted
causing you to slip
Those you gave into
after begging forgiveness
with parted lips"

For all women and men
The difference between
eternal light and dark
is related to the place
God occupies
in the heart

Retribution

You can cheat
You can lie
You can steal

You can connive
believing you've escaped
but know this for real,
That which you perpetrate
for premeditated advantage
at the expense and disregard
for one, for others
will be back to confront you
whether CEO or common shrew

Take note
be advised
as sure as the sun
tomorrow will rise
Someday you'll be honored
as the recipient thereof,
of retribution's revenge
cloaked in its love

Its vengeance exacted
for so long ago
Its Hydra heads providing
your payback apropos
Rewarding your past
selfish deeds
with identical
and more
updated seeds

A major or minor
responsibility misplacement?
Or conveniently forgotten
mental Rolodex file abatement?
Rest assured
and be dependently reliant,
those past offences
so brazenly committed
will return to force you
into compliance

For you will see
the eyes in the mirror
won't let you be
The ones behind the face
know and remember
each indelible denial
lurking in the background
awaiting revival

Rooms

Lonely at night
Lonely at noon
Stranded amidst this crowded multitude
manufactured by mind's eye
while confined in this room

Depression reigns supreme
living in a prone position
wondering if impending death
will make it
an easier transition

Unable to eat
Unwilling to move
Unfit to quell self-analysis
As mind's eye races
to insecure places

Waiting once more
to drift off to sleep

Sleep;
mind's eye room
within this other

Thoughts of you,
of what was,
of what might have been,
of that, which now
will never be

Safety only beneath
sweat soaked sheets
crumpled and soiled,
how apropos
life complete

The most effective diet
known to mankind
Depression-
total life; body and soul
held captive by misgivings
and trapped insecurities,
within mind's eye

Pulsating circle
of vibrating hum
gaining shape and size
Alternating betwixt
concave and convex
pummeling reduced growth

Praying, Asking
one to devour the other
and take me with it

Seen only by mind's eye

Second Hand Smoke

When you smell
like nicotine, tobacco and tar
from six to eight feet afar
we can pretty well guess
or at least estimate
you may be smoking too much
and you'd best hope
it's not too late

Stop Smoking
or at least smoke less, only a few
Maybe one, maybe two?
So the rest of us
don't find ourselves
gasping for air
as we stand next to you

Sharing the World

The old bridge sags
under the weight of age
A path leading to it
erupts from the forest
of earthen green
As endless foliage dominates
this Eden scene

Beaten hard and compact
from countless numbers
of pounding feet having tread past
not a single blade of grass
can establish and declare itself claimant,
as the last

Dirt muted mauve
with a darkened tinge of red
the two meld together
in a blackened three foot bed
Lying back
Looking skyward
Path asks for rain,
for dew
for damp
for moisture of any gain

To be resurrected once more
becoming darker still
and from its bordered edge to spill,
widening
to take on forest's growth
A continuous battle
of which, can expand the most

Lolling and calm
and wet is creek
Bubbling a murmur of life
reminding the others
of its presence beneath

Beneath bridge, creek is knelt
this watery interlope
waiting for rain
for deluge
for flood,
Requesting arrival
from streams up above
That once more it might rage
making its presence felt

Between these
still life three
Anchored, is the old bridge
Sagging from the weight of old age
determined in its place to stay
as path and forest and creek
challenge each other
day after day

She Said

"Here comes
the good stuff,"
she said
Almost in a whisper
just loud enough
to hear

Free sample
given and received
Time spent
on her knees
Cool kisses
fresh as a breeze
Oh how that girl
could tease
and please

Fireman's cap
highly exposed
cocked, loaded
ready to explode

Ever so slowly
with her brass ring
Around his maypole shaft
did she sing

Enjoyment from thumbs
fingertips
body parts
She titillated,
even his heart

From head to toe
and back again
she left his heads
in a spin

She was one
who knew her stuff
Never too little
just enough
Almost in a whisper
just loud enough to hear
leaning against him on the bed,
“Here comes the good stuff,”
she said

Someday

So you live in a world
full of fools
idiots in a rut
stooge upon stooge,
while you exist perpetually
in a strictly cool groove

Your habitual recurring thought
the one which arises
most often
of which you constantly think
is, after all
"my shit doesn't stink"

Now imagine,
you're stripped naked
laid bare to the soul
and stand to face
each of those
you arrogantly damned and chided,
blasted and derided,
self righteously demeaned,
with all those past thoughts
in your head
The ones in your mind
you violently screamed
But were too insecure to avow
out loud

Stranded in front of them
This assemblage of heaven
watching
with eight hundred billion
other pairs of eyes
at the big screen TV,
one as big as the sky

While the images
of your past
Your relations with your fellows
come streaming by
and you see yourself bellow

The name calling
The immature bawling
The dirt and filth
mentally cast at them
within your self-pitied gloom,
the foul thoughts and deeds
you cursed down upon them
as you ranted and raved
while isolated in the security
of your private room

Then, way back when
You, so selfishly proud
Now, with head hung down
silently
you wish, hope and pray aloud
As each and every
malicious intent and utterance
you ever had
is seen, read and heard
by heaven's gathered crowd

Now what?
How big do you feel?
How superior?
How aloof?

Now do you understand truly
What you were trying to prove

Who you really intended to hurt
The one you wished to ground
into the dirt?
You

Stone Washed Genes

Man's desire?
Cast his name in stone
Set his world afire

Woman's quest
Support his dreams
Provide for his rest

His ego
gets in his way
Her strength
helps him face
another day

He struggles
convinces
connives
and dies

She provides
to please,
and welcomes his release

Strain and Complain

Listening to the voice
inside my head
hearing lamentations
of dread and pain
anguished cries
like unrelenting rain

Tears running unabated
You now, so hard so hated
Flooded by emotions
Psychologically torn asunder
Physically a total wreck
since you've moved on

You said six weeks
was all you needed
uninterrupted and solo

As the hours creep by
and feel like years
The voices echo
with insecure fears

Believing you had
nothing to lose
You couldn't be honest
you couldn't be true

your thoughts;
no one saw or knew

From your selfish game
the truth won't be hidden
no matter how large
no matter how small
Responsibility resides
often enough
with he who looks
for someone else to blame

Terrible Too's

There are many today
going through the terrible too's
They kick, they scream
they spit, they spew
Wanting it all
wanting it now
"no restrictions, no waiting"
hear them howl

Refusing to listen
Unwilling to hear
they've made up their minds
for them it's quite clear
Ignorantly claiming
they have 'no fear'

Sans a plan
all ahead, full speed
with actions bold
no negativity possible
driven on by infallibility
they're ready to go

Perhaps, we should believe them
trusting they know of what they say
for they own the T-shirt
and have the funds
needed to pay
attorneys and bail bondsmen
who make substantial livings
from those still going through,
the terrible too's

Seeing others do it
expressly for thrills
motivation enough
attempting to prove
their Junior High antics
and braggadocios skills

No matter their age
they simply refuse
to grow up and out
of the terrible too's

Thought Train

The train pulls into the station
gliding silently through the depot
for it never truly stops,
it slows

Effecting a crawl to halt
but not

Appearing stationary in its place,
A more focused inspection reveals
movement

Staring down slightly
to extricate the luggage
from its position on the landing
Straightening
to step forward
the entry has edged away

Precipice thoughts
which had taken hold,
clinging
oh so briefly
are up-rooted
and grasped disjointedly

as the train moves
toward derailment

Thank Yous

Thank you Lord
for allowing me to struggle
with your Word
with your Will
with your Ways
That I may no longer struggle
with those of my world
this new day

Mahalo for allowing me
to wait upon your ways
that I no longer carry
upon these small shoulders
the weight of the worlds
I once did crave

Danke Schoen for allowing me
to come before you
that I might kneel
in reverence to your will
That from this day forth
my heart be
newly filled

Merci Beaucoup for allowing me
to know better your word
that those I so selfishly vent
might become mute
for their irrelevance

Gracias for allowing me
a heart and mind
filled with your presence,
to understand
I am not alone
in this time and place
and never have been

Arrigato for allowing me
to come back this time
As if I'd never left your side
for you, have never left mine

Thank you Lord
for remembering me
That I might never forget you

The Trough

Facing each other
at the trough
Standing knee deep
in their slop
Two twin hogs of
"it's all about me"
immature celebrity
and over ripened vanity

Smiling each broadly
from snout to snout
Growing ear-ward
east and west
Cynical sneers
behind pearly whites
Each believes
he is the best

Eyes twinkle brightly
with self deception
Begrudging acknowledgment
of each other's presence
Their ploys and practice
tricky tactics,
A plan to mount;
how to cut the other
down and out

Stone hard stares
between these two shared
Enmities of sloth
No matter the toes stepped on
No matter the cost

How to rig pomposity
How to cover hypocrisy
Remembering always,
There is no such thing
as bad publicity

Twin Towers

We come into the world
knowing
We are not aware however
that we know
Hence, our struggle begins

Consciousness from His breath
Conscience from His fingertip touch
Knowledge, our sole connection to God
is carried over
and brought forth with us,
from the light
into the darkness
Hence, our struggle begins

It is here, in this time and place
the kernel,
that seedling of ethic
is watered by
guilt
shame
embarrassment
Hence, our struggle begins

Conflicts rage past
as do the years
played out within our
choices
decisions
responses
to people and events that shape
the Twin Towers of our struggle,
Right and Wrong

Two Sided Coin

God allows struggle
turmoil and strife
that we may find opportunities
to remember He's there,
and here
We take baby steps
then over-powering strides
upon the paths
of smiles and tears,
which stretch before us
in this physical experience
we label life

Why, we ask
Why not, He replies
Would you that I
would not test all your lies
Since the beginning
when Adam ran and hid
and then blamed Eve
for the thing he did
Mankind has always
wanted a free ride
and that's why all of you
still run and hide

You refuse to realize
what you do
think and say
I always see
It's impossible to keep
your behavior from me
That's why I made the devil
the frightening and evil side
After all,
isn't that the point?

You each must choose
who will you serve
and please
We both will reward you
for whom you follow
and believe
his, eternal separation
from my eternal peace

What

“What”!
“Your presence eclipses
my field of vision”
“*What*”?

Woman's Day

Young men look outward,
world's to conquer
a mark to make
a claim to stake
Setting themselves
above all others
adamantly avoiding
potential blame
Making it perfect
according to plan
that's the way to be
a real man's man
Wondering always
what the world may think
as they live
close to the edge,
right on the brink

Old men look inward
wondering when
where
and why
so many of their plans
went so far awry
Having risked all their lies
on how it appeared
to so many others,
friends, enemies
competition, lovers

Young women confide
in their small circles
traumas; pre and post,
which of today's mistakes
will cost them the most
Appearance and Status
reign supreme
never must there be a pause
Without these two cornerstones
a young woman's life,
is as good as lost

Mature women know,
know and have lived
through problems
trials and troubles
All require
that they give
more of themselves
than ever expected
in thought
or in fact
Endless streams
of blood, sweat and tears
all shed,
throughout the years
Attempts to keep
those bursting bubbles
of their young and old
painlessly intact

Worlds

This world is of merit,
of 'good and bad' works
The spiritual world
universally surrounding
beyond and above
is simply about
truth and love.

You of this world
so concerned
about you and you alone
in this time and place
And yet, when it involves
the hereafter
your obsession is
with everyone else,
where they may be
eternally,
and why.

Those of self righteousness
remove the blinders
from your eyes.

Focus on your relationship
with God
Let Him be concerned
with all the others.

For He loves them
as they are,
The same way He loves you,
as you are.

XYZ Lamentations

Talking incessantly
sounding like chicken cackle
sharing Rice Krispies
Snap, Pop, Crackle

"On the clock?"
"We're still on break"
both spat back
arousing their hackles

"Stealing time is stealing money"
"We don't care"
they contemptuously spewed
"Our employers are
the hound and the jackal"

"We work by the hour
and their time is our money"
in unison two together groaned
as if bound and shackled

"They shouldn't expect us
to actually come in and work
For the wages we get
this job is too tough
They're plain lucky
we show up."

Young Love

Oh,
to be so innocent
and once again
think we know it all.
Love dies
when familiarity grows bold.

Other books by Branch Isole

SEEDS OF MANA'O ©
Thoughts, Ideas and Opinions in Poetic Prose
ISBN 0-9747692-1-5

BARKING GECKOS ©
Stories and Observations in Poetic Prose
ISBN 0-9747692-2-3

God. . .i believe ©
Simple Steps on the Path
of Spiritual Christianity™
ISBN 0-9747692-0-7

Order books by Branch Isole at
www.manaopublishing.com
Questions, Comments; go to our website
and click on the 'contact' link.

Living on the island of Maui, Branch Isole
is the 'voyeuristic poet' who shares Mana'o *
and God's Word in writing and with
individuals and groups visiting Hawaii.

Branch also writes poetry, articles and short
stories for journals, magazines, newsletters and
on the Internet at www.manaopublishing.com

* *Mana'o* (pronounced Ma Na O) is Hawaiian
for 'Thoughts, Ideas and Opinions'

www.ingramcontent.com/pod-product-compliance
Lightning Source LLC
LaVergne TN
LVHW091011080826
845145LV00003B/1218